TURN

2

HEALTHY
EATING

TURN
2
HEALTHY
EATING

A GUIDE BOOK FOR
BASEBALL STUDENT ATHLETES

SPENCER MUIRHEAD

TURN 2 HEALTHY EATING
A GUIDE BOOK FOR BASEBALL STUDENT ATHLETES

iUniverse books may be ordered through booksellers or by contacting:

iUniverse
1663 Liberty Drive
Bloomington, IN 47403
www.iuniverse.com
844-349-9409

Because of the dynamic nature of the Internet, any web addresses or links contained in this book may have changed since publication and may no longer be valid. The views expressed in this work are solely those of the author and do not necessarily reflect the views of the publisher, and the publisher hereby disclaims any responsibility for them.

Any people depicted in stock imagery provided by Getty Images are models, and such images are being used for illustrative purposes only. Certain stock imagery © Getty Images.

ISBN: 978-1-6632-1410-2 (sc)
ISBN: 978-1-6632-1421-8 (e)

Print information available on the last page.

iUniverse rev. date: 12/16/2020

This book is dedicated to my dad.
There aren't enough words to describe the best supporter.

INTRODUCTION

In baseball, as a player, you are not able to control a lot of things about the game. You cannot control whether or not you will get a fastball to hit in your hitting zone during your at bats. You cannot control whether or not the umpire will call borderline strikes. You cannot control whether or not the coach will put you in the lineup on a particular day.

But there are a few things that you can control. You can control your determination level. You can control how hard you work on the baseball skills. You can control the foods you are eating.

In my experience, players tend to focus a lot on the first two "controllables" and tend to neglect the third one. I don't think this happens because they don't want to manage their overall nutrition. Rather, I believe a large number of players don't know how to address the concept of healthy eating. They may know what foods are good for them but they may not know how to prepare the food to get the best nutritional value out of the food or they may not know when to eat the foods. I was in that boat at the beginning of my college career.

In high school, I was eating healthy and felt as though I had a good grasp of what to do. However, the jump from high school to university was different in that the school schedule was a complete contrast to what I had previously experienced. Classes would be at different times. Workouts were not happening at a consistent time each day. Not having a consistent and structured schedule made it challenging to manage the full process of shopping, cooking and meal prepping. My nutrition improved towards the end of my collegiate career once I discovered solutions to problems that I was running into.

My reason for writing this book is to help baseball student athletes find solutions to potential problems regarding healthy eating and meal prep. School can be tough and stressful but determining what you should eat and what to make for meals should not be an added stress in your life.

I will introduce you to three fictional college players - Joseph, John, and Tom. You may see yourself in one or more of these players. Each player is different in terms of body type, playing style, and reasons for wanting to reach a goal. For each player, we will look at their previous eating habits, issues they are running into, and strategies to overcome some of their problems.

This book is not a "cookie-cutter" solution to healthy eating. Everyone has different needs and has different experiences and schedules. What might work for one person will not necessarily work for another. Finding what works for you is really important so that you can succeed with healthy eating.

The recipes in this book are easy to prepare and, more importantly, they are affordable. Whether you are a freshman trying to figure out meals for yourself on a consistent basis or a junior looking for new recipes or a high school student looking to get ahead of the curve by finding recipes that work for you, this book will help you.

If eating the right way were to help your performance on the field, in the weight room, and in the classroom, would you do it?

One hundred percent you would. So let's look at what you can control in baseball as a student athlete.

MEET THE PLAYERS

Joseph

Joseph is a 6 foot 2, 170 pound sophomore outfielder. He has a thin, lanky build. Joseph gets into the lineup consistently because he is an above average runner and has good arm strength. He struggles to produce consistent, hard contact against good pitching (high velocity) at the plate. When he makes contact against good pitching, it is either a ground ball or a lazy fly ball. The ground balls he is hitting don't have enough speed to get through the infield and result in outs. Following the conclusion of his fall season, Joseph decides that he wants to look at gaining some muscle in order to produce harder contact. Joseph thinks he should aim to gain about 10-15 pounds before the start of the next spring season (3 month time frame).

From a dietary standpoint, Joseph eats a fairly well balanced diet of carbohydrates, protein, and healthy fats. (Along with water, carbohydrates, protein, and fats are the four macronutrients that are very important to our overall health). Joseph drinks around 1-2 litres of water a day. He believes he should be drinking more water but is unsure about how to increase his water intake. Joseph is a very active individual who works out for an hour and fifteen minutes each day. In addition, he will go and work on his baseball skills daily (hitting, throwing, etc.) and will play another recreational sport in the evenings as often as he can depending on his schedule. Joseph notices that in the afternoons, he will start to feel tired and will look for a snack (chocolate bar, chips, cookies, etc.) at the school's vending machine. In the past, Joseph has struggled to gain weight.

Problems

- Insufficient water consumption
- Tiredness in the afternoon
- Not consuming enough calories to accommodate his high activity level

Solutions

Joseph consults with his doctor and it is determined that he is healthy and can safely put on some muscle. He decides to consult with a Healthy Eating & Weight Loss Specialist because of his past experiences of not being able to put on weight.

For Joseph to achieve his goal of gaining weight and muscle, he needs to be in a caloric surplus. This means that Joseph needs to eat more calories than he burns off.

Because of his high activity level, Joseph needs to consume more calories. When he tried to gain weight in the past, the amount of food and number of calories he was consuming was getting used up throughout the day during his activities. Since his consumed calories were being burned though exercise, Joseph was unable to gain weight in the past.

In order to gain weight, Joseph should look at eating more carbohydrates. The main function of carbohydrates is to provide a source of energy. Carbohydrates can be found in a variety of different sources including baked goods and processed foods. The best carbohydrate choices for Joseph would be whole, natural, unprocessed and high fiber carbohydrates.

Joseph is familiar with the basic carbohydrates such as rice, pasta, and bread. He is surprised to learn that there are other carbohydrate options that can help him reach his goal. Other foods with carbohydrates include fruits, vegetables, legumes, and, nuts and seeds. The table below gives more examples of carbohydrates.

Vegetables	Fruits	Legumes	Nuts and Seeds
Bell peppers	Raspberries	Kidney beans	Almonds
Cauliflower	Oranges	Chickpeas	Cashews
Onions	Avocado	Lentils	Peanuts
Broccoli	Strawberries	Quinoa	Pumpkin seeds
Sweet Potato	Apples	Black beans	Sunflower seeds
Cucumbers	Bananas		
Spinach	Watermelon		

Through his research and reading, Joseph learns that generally, for people who are trying to gain weight, their daily food breakdown should be as follows:

- 40-45% calories from carbohydrates
- 25-30% calories from protein
- Remaining percentage from healthy fats.

Joseph thinks it will be challenging to increase his calorie intake. He is unsure if he will be able to do it. A potential way that Joseph can get those extra calories and carbohydrates is by drinking smoothies because they will help increase his carbohydrate intake. He should have a smoothie every couple of days with a meal. It is important to note that the smoothies will not replace his meals. Having smoothies are only a means of getting

3

more calories. Eating actual meals should be the goal for all athletes. [See the Recipe section for smoothie options.]

To help address Joseph's tiredness in the afternoon, in addition to eating more, he should bring snacks to school. In his case, he will want to pack higher calorie snacks such as nuts and seeds.

Nuts and seeds are good snack options because they contain a lot of calories per serving. Some good choices that Joseph can eat include pumpkin seeds, almonds, pistachios, cashews, and pecans. [See the Recipe section for a trail mix and seed mix recipe.]

Joseph just doesn't want to gain weight, he wants to build strength. To help his body recover from workouts, Joseph needs to consume protein. Protein provides amino acids which will help his muscles recover following a workout. Joseph should aim to consume complete sources of protein - food sources that provide all the essential amino acids. Joseph learns that there are twenty amino acids the human body needs to function optimally. Amino acids are like the building blocks for proteins and help with many different functions within the human body.

Of those twenty amino acids, there are eight essential aminos that need to be consumed through our diet. (**Note**: some sources say there are nine essential amino acids, but we will leave that debate for the scientists). Complete sources of protein contain all the essential amino acids. Examples of complete proteins include chicken, eggs, tuna, and ground beef. There are incomplete sources of protein that Joseph can also eat to get protein but he would need to combine different incomplete sources together to get all of the essential amino acids if he wanted a meal that was complete in its protein. For people who are vegan or vegetarian, they need to ensure that the foods they are eating have good protein sources that will provide them with the essential amino acids they need.

Joseph would be able to get some of the healthy fats he needs through different sources such as salmon, cheese, avocado and nuts. If Joseph is eating the right foods (whole, natural, unprocessed), then he will be able to get the appropriate amounts of healthy fats needed.

To address the issue of needing to drink more water, Joseph can look at a few different options. He could get a reusable, portable water bottle that holds a large amount of water. If Joseph only needs to refill the bottle once or twice during the day, then he will know that he has consumed the right amount of water for the day. Just as he has to replenish his calories after workouts, Joseph will need to replenish his water after exercising.

Joseph knows that water is essential. It hydrates the body and this is very important for athletes. Generally, Joseph should consume 2-3 litres of water per day in order to be well hydrated. However, due to Joseph's activity level, he will need to drink more water to help his body stay hydrated. If he is moving around (working out, practicing, or playing games), he will most likely be sweating and therefore, will need to drink more water.

Another strategy that Joseph can use to increase his water intake is to keep track of the amount of water he is drinking. By tracking his water intake, Joseph can hold himself accountable for drinking enough water. If Joseph didn't consume his needed amount of water for that particular day, then it should motivate him to work harder to drink more water the next day. Finally, having reminders, whether they are on his mobile phone or on sticky notes, will help keep Joseph on track to drink enough water.

For Joseph to be successful in reaching his weight gain goal, it will involve a lot of commitment and hard work. Achieving his goals will not happen overnight. It will take Joseph time and he will have to try to focus daily on eating right and working out effectively.

John

John is a 6-foot, 235-pound freshman corner infielder. John has a bigger build with some strength. He does not play every day as he platoons with the other first baseman on the team. John produces a lot of hard contact and gets extra base hits - just missing hitting home runs. On the field, John is a solid defender but he is not the most agile. As a result, he only plays first base. Over the course of the season, John realizes that he isn't able to score from second on hard hit singles and he doesn't always get ground balls hit to the sides of him. In addition, John knows that the current third baseman is graduating and he believes that he can play third base and get in the lineup more consistently next year. With that being said, John has determined that he needs to lose some body fat to improve his performance. His goal is to get a consistent starting spot in the lineup next year. John believes losing 10 pounds would be beneficial for him. He will be looking to attain his goal over the summer before heading back to school for the fall (4 month time period).

John's eating patterns are relatively well balanced. However, he tends to eat more carbohydrates such as breads and grains. John eats at fast food restaurants 5-6 times a week because of his busy schedule. He does eat protein but he is a little bored with his diet because he is eating the same meals week after week. John drinks about 2-3 liters of water a day but he notices that he will get muscle cramps every now and then especially when playing in hot temperatures and occasionally when he is working out at the gym. In terms of his activity level, John primarily spends his time in the batting cages. He hits every day for an hour. John does workout at the gym but only 3 times a week.

Problems

- Eats at fast food restaurants frequently
- Tired of eating the same protein sources
- Will experience cramping during exercise or during games

Solutions

John consults with a doctor who confirms John is in good health and can safely lose 10 pounds. He decides to consult with a Healthy Eating & Weight Loss Specialist as it is the first time in his life that he has decided to lose weight/body fat.

For John to lose weight/body fat, he will need to be in a caloric deficit. A caloric deficit means that John needs to consume fewer calories than what he needs to maintain his current weight.

To safely lose weight, John should look to lose a half a pound a week or a pound every two weeks. This amount of weight loss per week will ensure that he is not going into an unhealthy caloric deficit.

An important consideration for John is that he will need to consume the calories that he will lose from working out. If John does not consume the calories that he lost from his workouts, then he will potentially lose more weight than he intends. In addition, his muscle strength can suffer if John has a greater calorie deficit than needed as his body will look to his muscles for energy.

John did some research prior to his consultation with the Healthy Eating & Weight Loss Specialist and learned that to lose weight/body fat, he will need to eat more protein. John's research is correct. Consuming protein will ensure that he does not lose lean muscle or muscle mass. In addition, eating protein will keep John feeling fuller longer. Therefore, he should reduce the amount of food and calories that he will eat per day. Furthermore, protein will be less likely to be stored as fat by the body. Since John's goal is to lose body fat/weight, eating foods that won't be stored as fat will help him achieve his goal sooner.

Although John does eat complete proteins, he is getting tired of the same foods he is eating. A way for John to combat that issue is to start eating other options such as plant proteins.

Eating some plant proteins is a good way to change things up. Most plant proteins are not complete protein sources in that they do not contain all the essential amino acids. To get a complete protein source through plant proteins, multiple foods will need to be combined. There are a few different categories of plant proteins - legumes, nuts, and seeds. Below are some examples of plant proteins.

- Lentils
- Kidney Beans

- Black Beans
- Chickpeas
- Peanuts

Although John's goal is to lose weight/body fat, he will still need to eat carbohydrates so as to replenish glucose stores after working out and to provide his body with energy. John should look at consuming more complex carbohydrates rather than simple carbohydrates.

Simple carbohydrates are digested quicker than complex carbohydrates. As a result, they provide energy sooner because of their fast digestion rate. Eating simple carbohydrates would be ideal if John were to be physically active for a short period of time (i.e. a one hour workout).

Complex carbohydrates are digested slower (over a longer period of time) when compared to simple carbohydrates. Complex carbohydrates are good foods to eat if John were to work out over a longer period of time (2-3 hour baseball practice). Overall, if John eats more fruits and vegetables as his carbohydrates instead of breads, then his weight loss may be achieved sooner.

John's schedule will determine what type of carbohydrate he has to eat. A consideration for John is that if he plans on working out, then he will need to ensure that the carbohydrates he eats will be digested well in advance of his physical activity.

John also struggles with getting good meals on a consistent basis as his schedule is busy and he will turn to fast food options (restaurants, vending machines, etc.) 5-6 times a week to get food. This lifestyle can be problematic because of the type of fat John is getting from those meals. Foods that are highly processed tend to be high in trans-saturated fats or "trans fats." These trans fats can increase inflammation in the body which is not ideal for athletes and should be avoided.

Regardless of our goals, as athletes, we should look to consume healthy fats. John did not appreciate that there are healthy fats as he always associated fats with being "bad". The healthy fats that he should be consuming are monounsaturated and polyunsaturated fats. These two fats help improve cholesterol profiles, aid in heart health, and help with brain function.

Saturated fats are fats that should not be overly consumed because they can increase cholesterol levels. Saturated fats do have some benefits as they can boost the immune system and protect the digestive tract. However, it is important to limit the amount of saturated fats consumed per day.

To improve his overall diet and save some money, John should consider meal prepping. Essentially, meal prepping involves making meals a few days in advance. This helps people who are busy and are not able to make meals on a daily basis (most students and people working full time). Later on in this book, there is an entire chapter dedicated to meal prepping.

Finally, to address the issue of cramping during games or practices when in extreme heat or in the weight room, John should look to continue to drink a lot of water and should also look at drinking fluids with electrolytes - such as Gatorade®.

As athletes, we need water in order to help regulate body temperature when we are working out or playing in extreme heat. Playing in extreme heat or being dehydrated can cause muscle cramps which are not fun.

When we are sweating, we become dehydrated and lose electrolytes. This may cause cramping and other issues such as muscle weakness and fatigue. Although John is drinking water to stay hydrated, he isn't replenishing the lost electrolytes. So, by drinking fluids with electrolytes (Gatorade®), John will help improve his chances of not getting muscle cramps. John can also eat foods to help replenish his electrolytes such as watermelon and bananas which are both high in potassium.

In this particular scenario, since John is looking at losing weight/body fat, it would be recommended that he choose a fluid with less sugar. If John regularly drinks fluids high in sugar, then his progress towards his weight loss goal may be slowed down.

One key for John is to not get discouraged if he isn't seeing the results that he wants immediately. Losing weight/body fat can take time because everybody is different. The nutrition aspect will play a big role in John's ability to reach his goals. In addition, John will need to be working out and training on a regular basis to move towards his goals. If John is able to remain consistent with his training and with his nutrition, then he will see greater success in reaching his goals.

Tom

Tom is a 5 foot 10, 195 pound junior catcher and pitcher. Overall, Tom has a solid build. He has strength and can do a lot of things well on the diamond. Tom has an above average arm and he hits primarily for average. He plays well defensively. After his season, Tom feels as though he is at a good weight but feels he can improve his training and his nutrition. He is not looking to gain or lose weight. Instead, he is looking to improve every aspect of his game - baseball skills, physical strength, and nutrition.

Tom feels that where he needs to improve the most is in the area of his diet and he has made a strong commitment to himself to improve his diet. Tom eats well and his overall eating patterns consist of a well balanced amount of protein, carbohydrates, and fats. Tom skips breakfast fairly regularly as he is not particularly hungry when he first wakes up and he is not interested in cooking early in the morning. As a result, Tom will eat cereal in the morning along with a cup of coffee or tea. Tom knows that cereal from the store is not the best option but doesn't know what to eat in order to address his breakfast issue. In addition, Tom tends to get slightly hungry mid-afternoon and he is looking for good snack options. This afternoon hunger tends to hurt his performance when playing in double headers. When Tom gets tired, he will turn to a large coffee, tea, or soda to stay awake. Tom is a fairly active individual. He works out every day for at least an hour and will work on his baseball skills 4-5 times a week.

Problems

- Gets hungry in the afternoon which can affect double headers

- Drinks sugary drinks fairly regularly
- Does not eat breakfast

Solutions

In order to maintain his weight, Tom needs to eat the same number of calories that he has been previously eating. If Tom were to consume more or fewer calories than what he has been consuming, then he will either gain weight/body fat or he will lose weight depending on his activity levels.

Tom should continue to eat the same way in terms of getting a good balance of the macronutrients. One thing that Tom should consider is to ensure that he is getting an adequate amount of protein especially on the days he is working out or playing games. If Tom is diligent and mindful about consuming the necessary amount of protein per day, then he will continue to maintain his desired weight.

Skipping breakfast should not be something that is done regularly. Eating something in the morning will help provide energy for Tom. Not eating in the morning can cause Tom to feel tired later in the morning which can affect his classes, workouts, or games. Also, he could potentially over consume or under consume his calories for the rest of the day if he is not mindful.

To address Tom's issue of not wanting to cook food in the morning, a recommendation for Tom is that he make his breakfast food in advance. There are many options he could choose from in this book. The Spinach and Egg Omelette Casserole [see Recipe] could be eaten either cold or warmed up in a microwave. Another food option that can be made in advance is the Greek Yogurt Mix, a yogurt which provides protein and some carbohydrates and is also a good snack option. Tom can also prepare Breakfast Oats in advance. Breakfast Oats [see Recipe] is a meal option that has more carbohydrates than protein. If Tom wants to eat store bought cereal, then he should look at getting cereals that are whole grain or whole wheat. He should also make sure that there is not a lot of sugar in the cereal he is purchasing.

To help address the issue of being hungry in the late afternoon, Tom should look at a few different snack options to curb his appetite. Some good snack options that Tom can have are listed in the table below.

Chia Pudding	Cheese slices
Triscuit®, Veggies and Hummus	Trail mix
Roasted Chickpeas	Seed Mix
Fruit Cup	Turkey slices

Another recommendation for Tom would be to reduce the amount of coffee, tea, and soda that he is drinking. If he improves his snack options, then Tom shouldn't need to turn to caffeine to stay awake. Tom should continue to drink the necessary amount of water per day. Ideally, drinking plain water is the best source of hydration. If Tom struggles to drink water, he can also get water from other sources such as watermelon, lettuce, and broccoli. Beverages such as coffee, tea, soda, and juice should not replace Tom's water intake.

To reduce his hunger during double headers, Tom can look at a few different solutions. If he realizes he is hungry during the first game, then Tom can change what he has for breakfast. Tom can try the Breakfast Oats recipe. The oats in this receipe are a complex carbohydrate which will provide energy over a longer period of time because they are digested slower compared to some store bought cereals. If Tom has time in between batting practice and the game, he can look at having a snack. It will come down to his preference for a snack but a good option would be the Greek Yogurt Mix.

If Tom feels he is getting hungry during the second game of the doubleheader, then he should look at improving what he is eating in between games.

In addition, if Tom is trying to improve his overall nutrition, then here are a few other suggestions for him:

(i) Reduce his sugar intake. Eating foods with high sugar content should not be something that is done on a regular basis because those foods can increase blood sugar levels. Over time, increased blood sugar levels can potentially cause health issues such as Type II diabetes.

(ii) Plan his meals according to what he is doing on a particular day. This is partly associated with meal timing but for simplicity, here is an example. If Tom is not going to be very active for a day or two because he has a major exam and a paper due, then Tom could alter the type of carbohydrate he is eating for those two days. He could change to eating more complex carbohydrates instead of simple carbohydrates so that he doesn't overeat. That way, Tom doesn't consume more calories than normal and helps maintain his body weight. In contrast, if Tom is going to work out, he should be planning to eat a good pre-workout food and he should ensure that he has a good post workout meal with a complete protein source to help his body recover.

In Tom's case, the progress he is making with changes to his diet are subjective because his goal is to maintain his weight. This is important because Tom is judging how the changes in his eating patterns are making him feel. Tom will have to try different combinations of foods to know what makes him feel at his best for games, workouts, and during school.

HITTING A HOME RUN!

A good way to ensure that you are eating a well balanced diet is to meal prep. This section will show you how to maximize your time and efforts while meal prepping.

What is Meal Prepping?

Some people probably already know what meal prepping is because they are currently doing it or they know people who are. But there might be some players who do not know much about meal prepping.

Meal prepping is essentially making your meals ahead of time instead of making your meals on the day you eat them. The reason why meal prepping is done is so that you can pick your meals out of the refrigerator and eat them on the spot or pack them in your lunch. Meal prepping saves time for people who are either on the run or don't have time to make fresh meals every single day because of their schedule.

I started meal prepping during my last year and a half of university because the overall course load of almost all my classes was picking up and I felt that my nutrition levels were suffering because of it. I wasn't really able to make food the way I did in my first few years of university because I didn't have time. Luckily enough, I saw social media posts about meal prepping and I was pretty interested in doing the same thing so as to improve my nutrition levels.

Once I started meal prepping, I felt that I was more productive in terms of getting school work done because I wasn't thinking about what I was going to put together for my next meal. I also knew what snacks were available when I needed something in between meals. More importantly, I wasn't as tempted to buy a meal or snack from school because I was pretty proud of the meal I prepared. Not to brag, but I feel my meals taste better.

Although meal prepping takes time and effort, it is worth it. Meal prepping creates a sense of ownership over your nutrition. When you meal prep, you know exactly what is going into your meal and you can control the serving size.

How to effectively meal prep

From my personal experience, I have determined there are two key components to effective meal prep – *approach* and *execution*. Approach involves planning the meals, while execution involves actually preparing the meals. This can seem quite daunting especially if you have never meal prepped before. However, with a few tips, you will be able to effectively meal prep.

Approach

As baseball players we all know the importance of having an approach. When you are about to go up to bat, you should have an idea of what pitch you are looking to hit. For example, if you know the pitcher isn't throwing his breaking ball for a strike, then you most likely are not sitting curveball. You should be looking for a fastball. If you are looking for a fastball and your timing is on, then you have a greater chance of hitting a home run than someone who is looking for the curveball. The same concept of having an approach applies to your meal planning.

Hitting a home run doesn't just happen overnight. It takes a lot of practice. The same thing can be said about meal prepping. Creating meals and snacks doesn't come together in a few hours.

Planning to eat optimal meals can take days to figure out. From my personal experience, I know the best meals that I have made came from at least a few days of planning ahead. In contrast, I know that meals that were thrown together in a few hours of planning did not feel as complete from a nutritional standpoint because I know that I ended up missing a food group or an item that I wanted to have but ultimately ended up forgetting. It is a discouraging feeling to realize halfway through making a meal that you forgot to buy something.

To prevent this discouraging feeling from creeping in, I believe that writing down ingredients and or food that you want to eat for the upcoming week is very important. Let's say that your grocery shopping day is every Saturday. If you are updating a list everyday leading up to your shopping day, then you will be ready in multiple ways:

1. You will remember everything you need.
   - It is difficult to make/prepare complete meals if you don't have all the ingredients available to you.

2. You will stay focused and avoid impulse purchases.
   - Almost everyone has been there when they have gone shopping and think they have everything. You start to walk around making sure

you have everything and then that frozen pizza or those chips start calling your name. Next thing you know, you are purchasing them. Having a list will remind you to stay disciplined and not give in to those cravings and impulse purchases.

3. You will save time at the grocery store.
   - Trips will be shorter and once you know where everything is located in your grocery store, you won't be wasting time looking for where your items might be. Less time spent in the store means more time doing what you enjoy.

Something that will help you when you are preparing to go to the grocery store is planning what you will be eating for the following week. Let's say (hypothetically) in week one, your meals primarily consist of chicken, salmon, rice, and some vegetables. In week two (the following week), you do not want to eat chicken or rice and you decide to have meals that include steak bites, quinoa, lentils, and broccoli. If you know what you are planning on making for the next week, double check that you have the ingredients on hand to make those meals.

Execution (Putting it All Together)

Executing the meal prep can feel quite overwhelming even if you have been meal prepping for a long period of time. There are a few things you can do to make meal prepping easier to accomplish.

Before you begin cooking anything, make sure that the surfaces you are cooking on are clean. Those surfaces include the counter top, the kitchen table, the area around the stove burners, pots or pans that are being used to cook food and any bowls you might be using to mix ingredients. (When cleaning, I prefer to use Lysol® wipes.)

I've learned that the best way to start the meal prep is to cook any meats that you are making first. The main reason to start the process this way is that cooking the meats generally takes longer. So, while the meat is cooking in the oven, you can be preparing other foods. I will explain more in the next paragraph, but the main thing is that if you time everything right, then you should be spending less time in the kitchen. The second reason for cooking the meats first is that when the meat portion of your meals is done, you can let the meats stand and cool off while you finish cooking the other portions of the meal. This may seem kind of odd to let the food cool, but depending on what type of containers you are using to store the food, they can potentially break if they are going from hot to cold really quickly. This is primarily true for glass containers. I've seen it happen where glass breaks and trust me, no one wants to clean a fridge after just making fresh food. As a side note, if you are cooking multiple meats for the week, it can take more time to finish this section of the meal prep as most meats/protein sources do not always cook at the same temperature or they may require different prepping methods.

Once the meat portion of the meals is cooking, begin making the other components of the meals. This can include making vegetables, rice, or quinoa. These options should not take as long to prepare and cook compared to the meat portion of your meal. Once everything is prepared, the actual cooking portion of these meals does not necessarily take a lot of your time. You mostly have to monitor the food to ensure it is fully cooked.

Another thing to consider when preparing the other components of your meals is to cut up the food in advance. For example, if you are planning to have vegetables in your meals, then you can cut up the vegetables that you will be using the day before you cook. Another option is to buy pre-cut vegetables from the store. That option is a little more expensive but it has the potential of saving you time. The step of cutting the food in advance isn't mandatory. It just helps you save time during the cooking process.

After you have cooked all the food for your meal prep, you should line up the containers that you will be placing the meals in. I use takeout containers purchased from a grocery or kitchen store to hold the meals that I've prepared. Once the containers are lined up, add the appropriate amount of each food. The amount will depend on the goal you are trying to accomplish and how active you are. Add the meals to the containers and then load the containers into the refrigerator. Once this is done, you have successfully meal prepped. The only thing left to do is clean up. When you are taking the meals to school or to work, all you will have to do is heat the food up in a microwave - if that is your preference.

Glass jars such as Mason® jars can be used to hold/store a wide variety of foods and snacks. I only started incorporating glass jars into my meal prep fairly recently and I find them to be very beneficial. I have used these jars to hold breakfast meals, snacks, and salads. Creating these meals with the jars is not challenging but it can be time consuming. I would recommend preparing these jars after making your hot meals (chicken, vegetables, etc.). That way, you won't be overwhelmed with the cooking. Essentially, if you follow the cooking instructions and add the food in the specific order to the jars, then you will have meals and snacks ready to go for when you need them. A benefit of using jars is that you will be able to store some food in the refrigerator for up to a week. Therefore, you won't be throwing away food if you don't get to it right away.

When preparing meals for the week, you will need to meal prep at least twice a week because some foods do not have a long shelf life and need to be eaten within two to three days of being cooked. Your schedule will determine when you can allocate your time to making your meals. Snacks such as yogurt, chia pudding, or even the overnight oats can be prepared fairly quickly the day before you need them.

Things To Consider

If this is the first time you are meal prepping and you are getting overwhelmed, that's okay - don't panic. It will take some time to get a complete grasp on how to effectively meal prep.

In the initial stages, don't tell yourself that you have to do everything in the first week. You will become overwhelmed and most likely will get frustrated which can deter you from continuing.

Start small! Let's say you are in your first week of meal prepping. Have small, attainable goals. I would recommend that you set a goal of having a lunch meal for every school day of the week in a container. In addition, I would recommend preparing a snack for each day of the school week.

Once you feel comfortable with those goals and they become second nature to you, then you could add another goal such as making a container for dinner. It is a process that takes time to master. The main thing is to not get discouraged.

THE ESSENTIALS

In this section, I will be discussing some of the cooking essentials that you should have in your kitchen. For the high school student athlete, work with your parents if you need extra supplies. You probably have most of these things at home. For the college student athlete living off campus, assess your situation and determine what you need. Ask your parents if they have some spare pans and cooking dishes that you can take with you to college.

The Basics

Disinfecting Wipes/Spray

Using these wipes before cooking will help reduce bacteria and ensure that you are preparing your food on a clean surface. I use these wipes on the counter, kitchen table, and in the refrigerator... all the places where I will be cooking, combining the food for containers and storing the containers.

Glass Jars

For some of these recipes, you will be able to place the meal in a glass jar and store it in the refrigerator. The small/medium sized jars are great for storing yogurt, trail and seed mix, chia pudding, and breakfast oats. Pick up small to medium sized jars and see if you can find plastic, screw on lids for them. The metal lids are more challenging to clean and because you are not making preserves, you don't need the seal that the metal lid gives you. I have seen some people use large glass jars for salads.

Microwaveable Takeout Containers

You can use any kind of storage containers that you want (it depends on your preferences). However, I believe that the takeout containers are the best ones to use. I am not talking about the Styrofoam® containers that you may get from restaurants but the microwaveable containers that you can buy at wholesale stores or kitchen stores. I have had a set for 3 - 4 years and they are really durable. They don't break easily, are microwave safe and can be washed in the dishwasher.

Baking Sheets

Baking sheets will help you cook many different meals. A regular sized baking sheet (12 by 17 inches) is adequate for all the items you will be making.

- For easier clean up, I would recommend that you buy *aluminum foil* to lay over top of the baking sheet. Aluminum foil will help preserve the life of the baking sheet and will prevent you from scrubbing to remove the burnt contents of the food you made.

Frying Pans

I suggest having two frying pans. Having two will allow you to prepare more recipes at a time when you are meal prepping.

Small and Large Cooking Pot

I recommend bringing two or three pots with you so you can make multiple foods at the same time.

Strainer

For straining vegetables and pasta.

Casserole Dish

A casserole dish is very helpful to have on hand. Some of the recipes in this book require a casserole dish. A small to medium casserole dish would be more than adequate for one person.

Blender

If you plan on making smoothies, you will need a blender. Blenders can be expensive depending on the type you get. There are blenders that provide portable cups, which can be beneficial if you are trying to make a smoothie on the run. But a regular stationary blender works well to make up smoothies.

Other Items to Consider

Vegetable Steamer Basket

Ideally, we are supposed to consume vegetables either fresh or slightly cooked/steamed. Boiling vegetables can cause nutrients to be lost. The basket helps to prevent this from happening. It is not absolutely essential but it is something to consider. From personal experience, it takes a little longer to steam the vegetables because the basket that I was able to find only holds a small quantity of vegetables. To fill a few containers with vegetables, it takes me two or even three rounds of steaming vegetables to produce enough for a few containers.

Water Filter

Depending on where you live and the quality of your tap water, you might want to consider purchasing a water filter system. We have to drink a lot of water as athletes. Although the initial investment of a water filter can be sort of expensive depending on the model you get, in the long run, you will save money because you won't have to buy cases of bottled water. Also, for environmental reasons, you will reduce the plastic waste since you will use reusable water bottles. Personally, I have found the Brita® filter to be a good option.

Cheese Grater

In the long run, having a cheese grater will save you money compared to buying shredded cheese at the stores.

Food Scale

If you are tracking your food intake very closely, I recommend that you use a food scale. When you are tracking your food on an app, generally the app will ask for how many grams you ate. Having a food scale will help you with your calculations and tracking.

Lunch Bag

Try to find a good insulated lunch bag for your meal prep containers.

Ice Packs

An ice pack can help keep different foods cool and tasting better.

FIRST STEPS

I previously mentioned the need to have a grocery list before going to the grocery store. When I first began meal prepping, I was not entirely sure about where to start and what to buy. I had a general idea of what to do but I did not get everything I needed in the first trip to the grocery store. As a result, I was not able to hit the ground running.

The following food list will help give you a good starting base. You don't have to get all of the items on the list. You can pick and choose the options that you want to start with.

Some of these foods will last you a while (a couple of weeks) and will not have to be purchased on your next trip. Depending on what you make each week, you can store the uncooked food (chicken, ground beef, etc.) in freezer bags and put them in the freezer until the next time you want to cook them.

I suggest that you look at this list as well as the recipes that are in this book. If you see a recipe that you like, then write down those ingredients for your shopping list (if you need to buy them).

Please note that this is a very general list. If you have any allergies, medical conditions, or food sensitivities, please adjust your list accordingly.

Meats/Fish

- *Boneless, Skinless Chicken Breast*
- *Cans of Tuna*
- *Frozen Salmon Fillets*
- *Stew Meat*
- *Shrimp*

Fruits and Vegetables

- *Peppers*
- *Spaghetti Squash*
- *Onions*
- *Mushrooms*
- *Spinach (frozen and fresh)*
- *Garlic*
- *Frozen Vegetables (medley or individual types)*
- *Frozen Fruits (strawberries, raspberries, blueberries, or a medley)*
- *Bananas*
- *Raisins*
- *Fresh fruits (your choice)*

Legumes/Nuts and Seeds

- *Lentils*
- *Black Beans*

- *Sliced Almonds*
- *Almonds*
- *Cashews*
- *Sunflower Seeds*
- *Pumpkin Seeds*

Grains

- *Oats (steel cut or rolled oats and quick oats)*
- *Whole Wheat Rice*
- *Whole Wheat Pasta*
- *Tri-Color Blend Quinoa*
- *Chia*
- *Bread*
  - When choosing a type of bread, look for a whole grain or whole wheat or a whole grain loaf. Rye bread is another a good option.

Dairy products

- *Eggs*
- *Greek Yogurt*
- *Milk (choose from almond, soy, or regular milk- whatever you prefer)*
- *Cheese (personal preference)*
- *Cottage Cheese*
- *Sour Cream*

Spices/Seasonings

- *Salt*
- *Pepper*
- *Paprika*
- *Chili powder*

- *Oregano*
- *Granulated Garlic*
- *Knorr® Roasted Garlic and Herbs Pasta Seasoning*
- *Lemon & Pepper Seasoning*
- *Basil*
- *Parsley*
- *Crushed Red Pepper Flakes*

Other

- *Olive Oil*
- *Lemon Juice*
- *Vanilla Extract*
- *Maple Syrup or Honey*
- *Mayonnaise*
- *Granola*
- *Ranch Dressing*
- *Peanut Butter (or almond butter)*
- *Butter or Margarine*
- *Flax Seeds*
- *Dark Chocolate Chips (optional)*

RECIPES

RECIPES

In this section of the book, there are easy to make recipes. At the end of each recipe, there is a macronutrient breakdown that is rounded to the nearest whole number.

Most of these recipes are good to be stored in the fridge for two or three days. **Also, be mindful of allergies that you may have. Always read the labels and the ingredients before using or consuming.**

BREAKFAST RECIPES

GREEK YOGURT MIX

The yogurt mix has definitely been a game changer for me. This meal is a good breakfast option and can be a potential snack option. It has helped me curb hunger in between meals and has been a good pre-game snack as well. The yogurt can also be a good dessert if you add roughly 1 teaspoon of dark chocolate chips. You can also add bananas or granola.

I prefer using the frozen fruit with either a three or four berry mix. (I used the four berry mix for the macronutrient breakdown).

Ingredients (1 serving)

- 8 tablespoons Vanilla Greek Yogurt
- 2 teaspoons Sliced Almonds
- 1 teaspoon Flax Seeds
- 1/3 cup of Frozen Fruit (strawberries, raspberries, blueberries, or a mix of all)

Instructions

- Add the Greek Vanilla Yogurt to a medium size glass jar.
- Then layer in the following order: flax seeds; sliced almonds; your choice of frozen fruit.

Approximate Macronutrient Breakdown (1 serving)

Calories 278   Protein 23 g   Fat 5 g   Carbohydrates 33 g

BREAKFAST OATS

The Breakfast Oats recipe is a good alternative to cereal. This is a complex carbohydrate and should keep you fueled for a longer period of time compared to a processed cereal. One thing to consider is your fitness goal. If you are trying to lose weight/body fat, then make half the recipe and eat the oats along with another protein source such as scrambled eggs.

Ingredients (1 serving)

- 2/3 cup Oats (steel cut or rolled)
- 3 tablespoons of Chia Seeds
- 1 teaspoon Maple Syrup
- 2 - 3 tablespoons Frozen Fruit
- Raspberries
- Blueberries
- Enough milk to cover the oats (approximately 1/2 cup)

Instructions

- Add the oats and chia seeds to a medium size glass jar. Place a lid on the jar and shake it well to distribute the chia seeds. Add the maple syrup and the milk to the jar. Stir the contents.
- Add frozen fruit on top of the oat mixture.
- Place the lid on the jar and place in the refrigerator overnight so that the oats and chia seeds soak up the milk.

Approximate Macronutrient Breakdown (1 serving)

Calories 474   Protein 20 g   Fat 16 g   Carbohydrates 72 g

SPINACH AND EGG OMELETTE CASSEROLE

This recipe is a good way to get some carbohydrates and protein. Once this casserole is cooked up, it can be stored in the refrigerator and warmed up in the morning. If you would like to reduce the amount of fat in the recipe, you can reduce the amount of cheese or use a low fat cheese (part skim mozzarella).

Ingredients (4 servings)

- 1 cup Milk
- 1 pack frozen Spinach
- 3 Eggs
- 2 cups of Shredded Cheddar Cheese
- 1 teaspoon Salt
- ¼ teaspoon Pepper
- 1 cup finely chopped Red Peppers
- 1 cup of chopped Mushrooms
- ½ Onion finely chopped

Instructions

- Defrost the spinach and strain it.
- Pre-heat oven to 350 degrees Fahrenheit.
- Beat eggs in a mixing bowl.
- Add milk and cheese to the eggs.
- In frying pan, add a tablespoon of olive oil. Add the onions and mushrooms. Sauté for 5-7 minutes.
- Add the spinach to the pan. Continue to cook for 10 minutes. Add salt and pepper.
- Grease a medium size casserole dish with margarine (or with a vegetable spray).
- Add the vegetables from the frying pan, the eggs, and cheese to the casserole dish. Stir together until well mixed.
- Place in the oven and cook for 1 hour. Do not place the lid on the dish.
- Let it stand for 10 minutes.

Approximate Macronutrient Breakdown (per 1 serving)

Calories 268   Protein 24 g   Fat 16 g   Carbohydrates 14 g

EGG OATMEAL SCRAMBLE

A variation of scrambled eggs.

Ingredients (2 servings)

- 2 Eggs
- 1/4 cup Quick Oats
- 1/2 cup Milk
- 1/4 teaspoon Salt
- 1/2 teaspoon Vanilla Extract
- 2-3 teaspoons Maple Syrup or Honey

Instructions

- Beat the eggs in a mixing bowl.
- Add the salt, vanilla, oats, and milk.
- Coat frying pan with either butter or a vegetable oil spray to prevent sticking. Turn the element on to a medium heat.
- Add the contents of the bowl to the frying pan.

- Continuously move the mixture around until everything is cooked.
- Add the maple syrup or honey to the meal once removed from the frying pan.

Approximate Macronutrient Breakdown (1 serving)
Calories 323   Protein 20 g   Fat 14 g   Carbohydrates 32 g

LUNCH/DINNER RECIPES

RANCH CHICKEN SALAD

This chicken recipe is a good option for many different meals. You can make it for individual meals or you can add the chicken to a tortilla wrap or a burrito bowl.

Ingredients (3 servings)

- 2 Boneless Chicken Breasts (skinless)
- ½ of a small, chopped onion
- 2 tablespoons of Ranch Dressing

Instructions

- Cut the raw chicken breasts into fine bite-sized pieces.
- Add a small amount of olive oil to a frying pan and turn the burner on high heat. Add the chicken once the pan starts to get hot. Keep moving the chicken around the pan until fully cooked. Will take around 20 - 25 minutes to fully cook.
- Turn down the element and add some salt and pepper to the chicken. Let the chicken stand for 10 minutes.

- Add the chicken to a container and add the chopped onion and ranch dressing to the container. Mix the ingredients until well mixed.
- Store food you didn't eat in the fridge.

Approximate Macronutrient Breakdown (1 serving)

Calories 267   Protein 24 g   Fat 17 g   Carbohydrates 2 g

BASIC PARMESAN CHICKEN

This chicken recipe can be combined with almost any food to create a good meal. It's a complete source of protein and is very tasty.

Ingredients (makes 1 serving)

- 2 tablespoons of Mayonnaise
  - If you are watching your calories, choose the light mayonnaise.
- 1 teaspoon of Breadcrumbs
- 2 teaspoons of Parmesan Cheese
- 1 Boneless Chicken Breast (skinless)

Instructions

- Mix the mayonnaise, breadcrumbs, and Parmesan cheese in a bowl with a spoon until a good consistency is attained.
- Preheat the oven to 400 degrees Fahrenheit.
- Line a baking sheet with aluminum foil.

- Place chicken on the baking sheet. Spread the mayonnaise mixture on top of the chicken.
- Place chicken in the oven and cook for 35 minutes.

Approximate Macronutrient Breakdown (1 serving= 1 chicken breast)
Calories 392   Protein 42 g   Fat 13 g   Carbohydrate 2 g

SPICY CHICKEN

This chicken recipe may not be the hottest tasting chicken out there but it does have kick. If you are someone who doesn't like very hot or spicy food, then reduce the amount of chili flakes and paprika accordingly.

Ingredients (makes 3 servings)

- ¼ cup of Lemon Juice
- 1 teaspoon Black Pepper
- 1 teaspoon Paprika
- ½ teaspoon Garlic Powder
- ½ teaspoon Parsley
- ½ teaspoon Chili powder
- 1 teaspoon Salt
- 3 Boneless Chicken Breasts (skinless)

Instructions

- Mix all ingredients in a plastic bag. Shake the bag to coat the chicken.
- Keep the bag at room temperature for 10 minutes.
- Place aluminum foil on a baking sheet.

- Remove chicken from bag and lay on baking sheet.
- Preheat the oven to 425 degrees Fahrenheit.
- Cook chicken for 10 minutes.
- Keep the chicken in the oven and turn the heat down to 375 degrees Fahrenheit.
- Cook chicken for an additional 35 - 40 minutes.
- Remove from oven and let cool for 5 minutes.

Approximate Macronutrient Breakdown (1 serving)

Calories 230   Protein 42 g   Fat 3 g   Carbohydrates 9 g

BOURSIN® CHICKEN

I came up with this recipe after the Christmas holidays with the leftover Boursin® cheese. It is very tasty and easy to make.

Ingredients (1 serving)

- 1 Boneless Chicken Breast (skinless)
- ¼ cup of Pasta Sauce
- ¼ of a round piece of Boursin® Cheese
- 1 teaspoon Olive Oil
- ¼ teaspoon Black Pepper
- ¼ tablespoon Salt
- ¼ teaspoon Granulated Garlic

Instructions

- Preheat the oven to 350 degrees Fahrenheit.
- Line the bottom of a small casserole dish with olive oil.
- Place chicken in the casserole dish.
- Sprinkle chicken with black pepper, salt, and granulated garlic.
- Add pasta sauce to cover chicken.

- Divide the Boursin® cheese and place on top of chicken.
- Place chicken in the oven and cook for 50 minutes. Let cool for 5 minutes.

Approximate Macronutrient Breakdown (1 Serving)
Calories 486   Protein 47 g   Fat 35 g   Carbohydrates 8 g

LEMON & PEPPER CHICKEN

This might be one of the more basic chicken recipes in the book but it is definitely a good recipe to have on hand. There are not many ingredients involved which can allow you to quickly make this recipe.

Ingredients (1 serving)

- 1 Boneless Chicken Breast (skinless)
- ½ teaspoon of Lemon & Pepper Seasoning

Instructions

- Preheat the oven to 400 degrees Fahrenheit.
- Line the baking sheet with aluminum foil.
- Place chicken on the baking sheet.
- Sprinkle the Lemon & Pepper Seasoning on the chicken until covered.
- Bake in the oven for 35-40 minutes.

Approximate Macronutrient Breakdown (1 serving)
Calories 323   Protein 37 g   Fat 18g   Carbohydrates 0 g

ORANGE CHICKEN

This recipe is a good way to change up the chicken recipes. Combining this recipe with steamed or boiled vegetables would be a good option along with a side of rice.

Ingredients (4 servings)

- 1 tablespoon of Vinegar
- 1.5 tablespoons of Corn starch
- 1 tablespoon Soy Sauce
- 1 cup of Orange Juice (no pulp)
- 2 teaspoons of Brown Sugar
- 2 tablespoons of Hoisin Sauce
- 1 teaspoon Granulated Garlic
- 2 Boneless Chicken Breasts (skinless)

Instructions

- Chop up the two uncooked chicken breasts into small, bite-sized pieces.

- In a large mixing bowl, combine the orange juice, vinegar, brown sugar, hoisin sauce, soy sauce, corn starch, and granulated garlic. Stir until the liquid is a dark orange.
- Coat a large frying pan with olive oil or a vegetable oil and turn the element on to the highest heat. Place the cut up chicken in the pan and cook until done (no pink). This can take about 20-25 minutes to fully cook.
- Once the chicken is cooked, turn down the element to a medium-high heat and pour the sauce over the chicken.
- Continue to cook the chicken and sauce together on the medium heat. Keep the chicken moving around the pan to ensure that the sauce has coated the meat. You will have to do this for about 15 minutes. The sauce will eventually lose its liquid consistency and this lets you know the recipe is done.

Approximate Macronutrient Breakdown (1 serving = approx. 5 oz of chicken)
Calories 271   Protein 28 g   Fat 7 g   Carbohydrates 19 g

CHICKEN HUMMUS WRAP

Ingredients (1 serving)

- 1 Sliced Boneless Chicken Breast (skinless)
- 1 Whole Wheat Tortilla
- 2 tablespoon of Hummus
- 1 teaspoon of Salt
- 1/2 teaspoon of Pepper
- 1/2 teaspoon of Granulated Garlic
- One-half of a small Cucumber (chopped)
- Handful of Lettuce or Spinach (11 grams)
- Other veggies (your choice)

Instructions

- Place the sliced chicken breast in a frying pan with the element on high heat. Add a little olive oil to the pan to prevent sticking. Cook the chicken for 20-25 minutes. You will know that the chicken is cooked when there is no pink in the meat.

- Once cooked, turn down the element to a medium heat. Add salt, pepper, and the granulated garlic to the chicken. Stir the meat to evenly distribute the seasonings.
- Spread the hummus onto the tortilla. Add the chicken to the center of the tortilla. Add the cucumber, spinach, and any other vegetables you want.
- Fold the tortilla to create the wrap.

Approximate Macronutrient Breakdown (per 1 serving)

Calories 361   Protein 29 g   Fat 10 g   Carbohydrates 37 g

TUNA MELT SANDWICH

This is a good sandwich to have at any time either for lunch or dinner. Tuna is a very good source of protein and provides an option for getting good healthy fats.

Ingredients (makes 2 servings)

- 1 can of Tuna (I used a small can. Serving size might differ if using a larger can)
- 2 teaspoons of Mayonnaise
- 1 teaspoon of Relish
- ½ cup of Shredded Cheese
- 2 slices of Rye bread (or whole wheat)

Instructions

- Preheat the oven to 375 degrees Fahrenheit.
- Drain the can of tuna.
- Put the tuna into a bowl and mix in mayonnaise and relish. Stir until evenly mixed.

- Place rye bread on baking sheet. Spread the mixed tuna onto the bread.
- Shred cheddar cheese and place on top of tuna.
- Place in the oven for 8 minutes.
- Let stand for 5 minutes.

Approximate Macronutrient Breakdown (1 serving)
Calories 211   Protein 25 g   Fat 11 g   Carbohydrates 9 g

BEST SHRIMP

This shrimp recipe is extremely tasty and spicy and goes well with pasta. You don't have to warm up the meal after it has been cooked. With this recipe, you will need to add other side options to the meal. Good sides are rice, whole wheat pasta, vegetables, the vegetable mix, quinoa, or a salad. The only drawback to the recipe is that shrimp can be expensive. (I usually make it about once a month.)

Ingredients (makes 4 servings)

- 5 cups of frozen, cooked small to medium Shrimp (peeled, deveined, tail off)
- 1/4 cup Lemon Juice
- 2 teaspoons of Butter or Margarine
- 1 teaspoon of Granulated Garlic
- 1/2 teaspoon of Parsley
- 1/2 teaspoon of Paprika
- 1/2 teaspoon of Basil
- 1/2 teaspoon of Crushed Red Pepper flakes
- 1 teaspoon of Salt
- 1/2 teaspoon of Pepper

Instructions

- Place the shrimp in a frying pan on a stove top with high heat.
- Add the lemon juice to the pan. Keep stirring the shrimp to ensure the shrimp is cooked thoroughly.
- Once the shrimp are separated from each other, add the butter/margarine to the frying pan. Keep stirring the shrimp around the pan.
- Once the butter/margarine is melted, turn down the burner to a medium heat. Add the granulated garlic and stir.
- Add the parsley, paprika, basil, crushed red pepper, salt, and the pepper to the frying pan. Stir thoroughly to distribute all the spices.
- Let the pan simmer for 3-5 minutes at low to medium heat.
- Turn off burner and let stand for 3-5 minutes.

Approximate Macronutrient Breakdown (1 serving = 100 g of shrimp)

Calories 170   Protein 24 g   Fat 8 g   Carbohydrates 1 g

BASIC SALMON

Ingredients (1 serving)

- 1 fillet of Salmon
- 1 teaspoon Olive oil
- ½ teaspoon Salt
- Approx. 1/8 teaspoon of Pepper

Instructions

- Preheat the oven to 400 degrees Fahrenheit.
- Line the baking sheet with aluminum foil.
  - Place fish on baking sheet. Drizzle fish with olive oil. Sprinkle with salt and pepper.
- Bake fish for 20-25 minutes.
- Let stand for 5 minutes.

Approximate Macronutrient Breakdown

Calories 160   Protein 21 g   Fat 9 g   Carbohydrates 0 g

LEMON PEPPER SALMON

This is a very easy recipe to put together. If you have your vegetables and quinoa prepared, it makes a very easy meal.

Ingredients (1 serving)

- 1 fillet of Salmon (frozen or fresh)
- 1/2 teaspoon of Lemon & Pepper Seasoning

Instructions

- Preheat the oven to 400 degrees Fahrenheit.
- Place aluminum foil on baking sheet.
- Place the salmon on the baking sheet. Add the Lemon & Pepper Seasoning to the salmon.
- Bake the salmon for 20-25 minutes.

Approximate Macronutrient Breakdown (1 serving)
Calories 120   Protein 21 g   Fat 5 g   Carbohydrates 0 g

GARLIC BUTTER SALMON

Ingredients (1 serving)

- 1 fillet of Salmon (fresh or frozen)
- 1/4 teaspoon of Salt
- 1/4 teaspoon of Butter
- 1/4 teaspoon of Granulated Garlic

Instructions

- Preheat the oven to 400 degrees Fahrenheit.
- Place aluminum foil on baking sheet.
- Place the salmon on the baking sheet. Sprinkle the salt and granulated garlic on the salmon. Place the butter on the salmon.
- Bake the salmon for 20-25 minutes.

Approximate Macronutrient Breakdown (per 1 serving)
Calories 155   Protein 21 g   Fat 8 g   Carbohydrates 0 g

SMOKED PAPRIKA SALMON

Ingredients (1 serving)

- 1 fillet of Salmon (fresh or frozen)
- ¼ teaspoon Paprika
- 1 teaspoon Lemon Juice
- ¼ teaspoon of Salt
- Approx. 1/16 teaspoon of Pepper (sprinkle for flavor)

Instructions

- Preheat the oven to 400 degrees Fahrenheit.
- Place aluminum foil on baking sheet.
- Place the salmon on the baking sheet. Coat the salmon with the lemon juice, sprinkle the paprika, salt, and pepper on top.
- Bake the salmon for 20-25 minutes.

Approximate Macronutrient Breakdown (1 serving)

Calories 123   Protein 21 g   Fat 4 g   Carbohydrates 0 g

STEAK BITES WITH SOME KICK

Steak Bites with Some Kick is a really good meal for lunch. Add the bites, rice or quinoa and some vegetables to your takeout container and you have a good meal to take to school.

Ingredients (makes 4-5 servings)

- 2 packs of Stew Meat (about 17 oz. total)
- 1 -2 tablespoons of Olive Oil (amount may vary depending on the size of the pan)
- 1 teaspoon Parsley
- 1 teaspoon Pepper
- 1 teaspoon Chili Powder
- 1.5 teaspoon Salt

Instructions

- Place a frying pan on the burner and coat the frying pan with olive oil.
- Turn the element on to a high heat.

- Add the stew meat to the frying pan. Keep turning the stew meat over consistently (every 2-3 minutes) to fully cook the meat. This will take 20-25 minutes.
- Once fully cooked, turn down the heat to a medium heat.
- Add half the amount of the parsley to one side. Then flip the meat and add the remaining parsley.
- Do the same with the salt, pepper and chili powder and cook for 2-3 more minutes.

Approximate macronutrient breakdown (1 serving = approx. 3-4 oz.)
Calories 270   Protein 24 grams   Fat 20 grams   Carbohydrates 0 g

GROUND BEEF FRY

This recipe can be combined with a variety of different foods. You can add this to pasta, on top of the burrito bowl, or with vegetables. It is a tasty recipe that does not take too long to make. One consideration with this recipe is that you need to be monitoring the food over the entire duration of the cooking process. Ground beef is high in fat, so attempt to limit how often you have it.

Ingredients (6 servings) serving size will depend
on the amount of ground beef used

- Lean Ground Beef (2 packs equaling approx. total of 850 grams)
- ½ small Onion (chopped)
- 4 cloves of Garlic
- 1 can of Mushroom Soup (Small-medium can should be adequate. Will depend on how much you are making)

Instructions

- Chop up half of a small onion and the four cloves of garlic.

- Place a frying pan on stovetop and turn the element on to high heat. Add the garlic and onions to the pan.
- Place the ground beef in the pan. Break the ground beef up into smaller pieces. Keep moving the ground beef around to ensure the meat is fully cooked. Fry the beef at high heat for 25 – 30 minutes. **There should be no pink meat and juices should run clear.**
- Once the ground beef is fully cooked, turn down the element to a medium heat. Add the mushroom soup to the frying pan and mix it in with the ground beef. Keep moving the ground beef around to mix the soup in for about 10 minutes.

Approximate Macronutrient Breakdown (1 serving)

Calories 418   Protein 34 g   Fat 28 g   Carbohydrates 5 g

SAUSAGE AND VEGGIES

The Sausage and Veggies recipe is an easy way to cook both your protein and carbohydrates at the same time. Cutting up the vegetables is the more tedious part of making this recipe. Aside from that, once it's in the oven, you are able to focus on making other recipes for your meal prep.

Ingredients (makes 4 servings)

- 4 Sausages (you can choose the type i.e. mild, hot, etc.)
- 3 Red Peppers
- 1 Onion
- 6 cloves of Garlic
- 2 cups sliced Mushrooms
- 1 teaspoon Salt
- 1/2 teaspoon Black Pepper
- 1 teaspoon Paprika

Instructions

- Preheat the oven to 420 degrees Fahrenheit.
- Line casserole dish with aluminum foil.

- Chop up 6 garlic cloves and add to casserole dish.
- Add the sausages. Make sure they are not too close to each other.
- Chop up the mushrooms, onion, and peppers. Place them around the sausages.
- Sprinkle the salt, pepper, and paprika evenly over the food. You can add a small amount of olive oil to the vegetables for more flavour.
- Cover casserole dish.
- Cook for 65-75 minutes.

Approximate Macronutrient Breakdown (1 serving)

Calories 435   Protein 24 g   Fat 32 g   Carbohydrates 15 g

HEALTHIER PIZZA

Most people like pizza - and sometimes, we get a pizza craving. This recipe provides a way to satisfy that craving. As a suggestion, you can store the pita in the freezer and always have a couple of cans of pizza sauce on hand for when you may want some pizza. If you have shredded cheese and cold cuts on hand, you can have this alternative at any time.

Ingredients (makes 1 serving)

- 1 Whole Wheat Pita Bread
- 3 teaspoons Pizza Sauce
- 1/3 cup Shredded Cheese (pizza mozzarella or marble)
- 4 slices of Salami (or other cold cuts)
- Additional toppings (optional)
  - Mushrooms
  - Peppers
  - Tomatoes
  - Spinach

Instructions

- Preheat the oven to 350 degrees Fahrenheit.
- Line baking sheet with aluminum foil.
- Place whole wheat pita on baking sheet.
- Add pizza sauce and spread around the pita.
- Place shredded cheese on top of sauce.
  - Depending on preference, add as much or as little cheese as you like.
- Add your toppings (meat, vegetables, etc.).
- Bake for 10 minutes.

Approximate Macronutrient Breakdown (1 serving)

Calories 367   Protein 24 g   Fat 17 g   Carbohydrates 36 g

LENTIL BAKE

This recipe can either be the main meal or a side dish. I used a vegetable medley for the veggies. The macronutrient breakdown will be different for other vegetables used. The macronutrient breakdown will vary depending on the type of lentil you use.

Ingredients (4-6 servings)

- ¾ cup dry Green Lentils
- ½ small Onion (chopped)
- 1 can Tomato Soup (small to medium size can)
- 2 cups of Veggies (already cooked boiled or steamed)
- ¼ teaspoon Pepper
- ½ teaspoon Salt
- 1 tablespoon of Splenda®

Instructions

- To make the lentils:
  - Place the lentils in a pot with 1.5 cups of water. Boil the lentils on medium heat until cooked. (About 20 minutes)

- Once lentils are prepared, add them to a casserole dish. Add the vegetables to the casserole dish. Sprinkle with salt, pepper, and Splenda®.
  - You may need to spray the casserole dish with vegetable oil to prevent contents from sticking to the dish.
- Add the tomato soup to the casserole dish and stir the contents together to ensure the soup is evenly distributed.
- Preheat the oven to 350 degrees Fahrenheit and cook for 45 minutes.

Approximate Macronutrient Breakdown (1 serving)

Calories 407   Protein 25 g   Fat 2 g   Carbohydrates 79 g

BURRITO BOWL

This is a recipe to have when you want to switch things up a little. If you are trying to lose weight, reduce the amount of rice and beans you place in the bowl.

For the macronutrient breakdown, I used leftover steak. I attempted to put about 3 ounces of the steak in the meal. If you use another protein source, your macronutrient breakdown will be different. For simplicity, I did not include any of the optional toppings in the macronutrient breakdown.

Ingredients (4-5 servings)

- 1 cup Brown Rice (Can be replaced with quinoa)
- 1 can of Black Beans
- 2 Peppers
- 1 Onion (chopped)
- Shredded Cheese
- Salsa
- Romaine lettuce
- Meat (Fully cooked Chicken, Steak Bites, or Ground Beef.)
- Corn (optional)

- Avocado (optional)
- Sour Cream (optional)

Instructions

- Cook the brown rice in the oven at 375 degrees Fahrenheit for 40-45 minutes.
  - *How to bake rice*: In a casserole dish, add 1 cup of brown rice, 2 cups of water, ½ teaspoonful of salt, and 1 teaspoonful of margarine. Bake in oven at 375 degrees Fahrenheit for 40-45 minutes.
- Strain the black beans and heat in a small pot on a stove top at medium-high heat for 10 minutes.
- Cut up the lettuce, onions, and peppers and any other vegetables that you want to add. Make sure the vegetables are finely cut. You can either add them to the bowl raw or you can fry them in a frying pan for 10 minutes on high heat.
- You can either buy shredded cheese or you can shred the cheese yourself.
- Ensure that the meat portion of the meal is fully cooked.
- Once all the food is cooked, layer them in your bowl.
- Recommended layering
  - 1/4 cup of Rice
  - 1/4 cup Beans
  - Vegetables (1/4 cup Red Peppers, 1/4 cup Onions, 1 cup Lettuce)
  - 3 teaspoons of Shredded Cheese
  - 1 teaspoon of Salsa (and any other toppings you want)
  - Cooked meat

Approximate Macronutrient Breakdown (1 serving)

Calories 450   Protcin 37 g   Fat 15 g   Carbohydrates 40 g

VEGETABLE FRY

This recipe is a very good option for people who are looking to increase their vegetable intake. It is very easy to make once all the items are chopped up. These vegetables can be added to any meal. If you are looking at using this recipe in your meal prep, then you will need to add a lot of spinach to the frying pan because as the spinach is being cooked, it loses its water content and becomes very small. This recipe can be combined with some quinoa or rice.

Ingredients (3-4 servings)

- 3 Peppers
- 4 cloves of Garlic
- 2 cups of finely chopped Mushrooms
- 1 small Onion chopped
- 6 cups of Spinach (fresh)
- 1 tablespoon of Olive Oil (just enough to coat the pan)
- 1 teaspoon Paprika
- ½ teaspoon Salt
- ½ teaspoon Pepper

Instructions

- Finely chop up the peppers, mushrooms, onions, and garlic.
- Coat frying pan with olive oil. Turn the element of the stove on to a medium-high heat.
- Add the onions, garlic, and mushrooms to the frying pan. Fry them for 5 minutes. Add the peppers to the pan. Constantly stir the vegetables for 5-10 minutes.
- Add the paprika, salt, pepper, and the red pepper flakes to the vegetables.
- Once the veggies are cooked, turn the element down to a low-medium heat and add the spinach. Cook for 5 - 10 minutes.

Approximate Macronutrient Breakdown (1 serving)

Calories 86   Protein 4 g   Fat 4 g   Carbohydrates 12 g

SPAGHETTI SQUASH

This recipe is a good side option for practically any meal. The vegetable looks like spaghetti but is a healthier option that the traditional pasta. The seasoning that will be used can also be used for regular pasta.

Ingredients (3-4 servings)

- 1 Spaghetti Squash
- 1 packet of *Knorr® Roasted Garlic and Herbs Pasta Seasoning* - can choose another seasoning packet if you want
- 1/2 teaspoon Salt

Instructions

- Rinse off and wipe down the exterior of the spaghetti squash.
- Cut the spaghetti squash in half. Place the squash on the cut side down in a large casserole dish.
- Add 4 cups of water to the dish. Add a teaspoon of salt to the water.
- Pre heat the oven to 350 degrees Fahrenheit.
- Cook the vegetable for 1 hour and 15 minutes to 1 hour and 20 minutes.

- Once cooked, remove the seeds with a spoon. With a fork, scrape out the inside of the squash and place in a bowl. It should look like spaghetti when you remove the squash.
- Add the packet of seasoning to the squash and mix together. You can substitute the packet of seasoning for just salt and pepper if you want to change the flavor. You can also just serve with butter or margarine.

Approximate Macronutrient Breakdown (1 serving)
Calories 105   Protein 2 g   Fat 5 g   Carbohydrates 15 g

QUINOA BEAN SALAD

This is a very good recipe that can go well with other meals. You are getting a lot of plant protein in this meal.

Ingredients (makes 4 servings)

- 1 cup Quinoa (the Tri-Colour option is a good one to get)
  - To prepare quinoa: Boil 2 cups of water in a small pot. Add 1 cup quinoa to small pot and 1/2 teaspoon of salt. Turn down the heat of the burner to a medium heat and stir periodically until water is absorbed by quinoa. (Approximately 15 - 20 minutes.)
- 1 can Black Beans
- 1 can Unsalted Chickpeas
- 2 Red Peppers
- Feta Cheese (crumbled)

Instructions

- Heat up the black beans in a pot. You will need to strain the liquid from the can before cooking. Heat up for 5 - 7 minutes (medium heat).

- Strain the liquid from the chickpeas can and rinse chickpeas thoroughly.
- Chop up the red peppers into fine pieces.
- Layer the ingredients in the following order: 1/4 cup Quinoa; 6 teaspoons of Black Beans; 6 teaspoons of Chickpeas; Red Pepper slices; Feta Cheese (3 teaspoons).

Approximate Macronutrient Breakdown (per 1 serving)

Calories 380   Protein 16 g   Fat 8 g   Carbohydrates 47 g

BEAN SALAD

This is a good cold salad to have. Can be added to a wide variety of meals. All the cans of beans that were used were regular (medium) size.

Ingredients (6 servings)

- 1 can of Kidney Beans
- 1 can of Yellow Beans (wax beans)
- 1 can of Green Beans
- 2 stalks of chopped up Celery
- 1 small Onion (chopped)
- ½ cup Vinegar
- ¼ cup Vegetable Oil
- 5 tablespoons of Splenda®

Instructions

- Strain and rinse the kidney beans, green beans, and yellow beans under cold water.
- In a large bowl, add all the beans together.

- Rinse and chop up the two stalks of celery and add them to the large bowl with the beans.
- Add the vinegar, olive oil, and the Splenda® to the bowl. Stir well to coat the beans.
- Cover the bowl and place in the fridge overnight.

Approximate Macronutrient Breakdown (per 1 serving)
Calories 181   Protein 6 g   Fat 9 g   Carbohydrates 19 g

SNACKS

TRAIL MIX

If possible, have a trail mix made and ready go all the time. Trail mix is good to have on hand especially if you are at school because it is much better than the vending machine options. You can decide whether or not you want the different ingredients salted or unsalted. Going to a bulk food store will allow you to control how much you want to have and your price. If you want to save time, you can buy a ready-made trail mix from the grocery store. You don't have to eat this snack in one sitting. You can have portions of it throughout the day or over the course of a couple of days.

Ingredients (1 small glass jar)

- 2 tablespoons Almonds
- 2 tablespoons Cashews
- 2 tablespoons Peanuts (eliminate if there is an allergy issue among teammates or classmates)
- 1 tablespoon Raisins
- 1 teaspoon small/mini chocolate M&M's®

Instructions

- In a container or small sized glass jar combine the ingredients listed above.
- Shake the container well.

Approximate Macronutrient Breakdown (1 small glass jar)

Calories 505   Protein 16g   Fat 38 g   Carbohydrates 33 g

SEED MIX

Similar to the Trail Mix, this snack is great to have on hand.

Ingredients (1 small glass jar)

- 2 tablespoons Sunflower Seeds
- 2 tablespoons Pumpkin Seeds
- 1 tablespoon Raisins
- 2 tablespoons Walnuts

Instructions

- Add the ingredients to a small glass jar or container of your choice.
- Shake the container well.

Approximate Macronutrient Breakdown (1 small glass jar)
Calories 465   Protein 17 g   Fat 38 g   Carbohydrates 25 g

TRISCUIT®, VEGGIES, AND HUMMUS

You can either cut up your own veggies or you can purchase a veggie platter and then separate the vegetables into portable containers. If you are attempting to lose weight, you should look at reducing the number of Triscuit® crackers. The amounts listed below would fill up a take-out container. (Again, you don't have to eat everything in one sitting. I would recommend taking a container of vegetables with you to school or to a game so you have good, healthy alternatives available to you.)

Ingredients

- 8 Triscuit® Crackers (Original with Sea Salt)
- Vegetables
  - 10 baby Carrots
  - 6 pieces of Broccoli
  - 5 pieces of Cauliflower
  - 7 pieces of Celery
  - Can add other options as well
- Hummus or another dressing

Instructions

- Rinse and chop up the veggies.
- Place the veggies in a snack container. You will need to have a separate container for the crackers.
- Getting a pre-packed hummus snack container for the hummus makes it easier and less messy to carry the snack. (Alternatively, you can use a small storage container if you prefer to buy the hummus in larger quantities.)

Approximate Macronutrient Breakdown

Calories 419   Protein 14 g   Fat 11 g   Carbohydrates 66 g

CHIA PUDDING

This recipe is similar to the Breakfast Oats recipe except the chia pudding is ideal for a snack or a dessert. If you are looking to lose weight or body fat, the granola can be removed.

Ingredients (1 serving)

- 3 tablespoons of Chia Seeds
- 1/3 cup of Milk
- 2 teaspoons of Blueberries or other fruit (can be fresh or frozen)
- 2 teaspoons of Honey
- 2 tablespoons of Granola

Instructions

- Add the chia seeds to a small/medium sized glass jar.
- Pour the milk into the jar.
- Add the honey to the jar and stir together with the milk until well mixed.

- Add the fruit and the granola to the jar. Stir to mix well.
- Place in the refrigerator for a few hours before eating.

Approximate Macronutrient Breakdown (1 serving)
Calories 286   Protein 9 g   Fat 16 g   Carbohydrates 40 g

BAKED CHICKPEAS

This snack is very tasty and is a much better option than processed, store bought snacks. When making this recipe, make sure that you do not overcook the chickpeas, as it will become challenging to remove them from the baking sheet.

Ingredients (4-5 servings)

- 1 can of Chickpeas (regular size can)
- 1 teaspoon of Granulated Garlic

Instructions

- Preheat oven to 375 degrees Fahrenheit.
- Strain the chickpeas and rinse them thoroughly with cold water.
- Place aluminum foil on a baking sheet.
- Evenly distribute the chickpeas on the baking sheet.
- Evenly coat the chickpeas with the granulated garlic.

- Cook for 30 minutes.
- Once cooked, let cool and separate them into snack containers.

Approximate Macronutrient Breakdown (1 serving)
Calories 112   Protein 7 g   Fat 1 g   Carbohydrates 19 g

FRUIT CUP

Preparing this fruit cup can be a little tough. If you want to save time in the preparation, you can buy a fruit platter from the grocery store and then separate the fruit into smaller containers. You will need to keep this snack in the fridge to keep the fruit from going bad. If you are going to a game or practice, make sure to bring an ice pack to keep the food cool.

Ingredients (1 serving)

- 5 Strawberries
- 6 cubes of Honeydew melon
- 6 cubes of Watermelon
- 6 cubes of Cantaloupe
- Optional
  - Mango
  - Pineapple
  - Berries of your choice

Instructions

- If you buy a prepared fruit platter from the store, separate the fruit accordingly into a small-medium sized container.
- If you prepare the food without the help of a pre-made fruit platter, then make sure to wash all the fruit you use. For the melons, rinse and wipe off the outside of the melons before cutting.
- Cut off any stems from the strawberries, slice the watermelon, honeydew, and cantaloupe into bite-sized pieces. Once the preparation is done, combine in a small to medium sized container.

Approximate Macronutrient Breakdown (1 serving)

Calories 155   Protein 2 g   Fat 0g   Carbohydrates 39 g

OTHER SNACK IDEAS

These options are pretty easy to assemble and they are sometimes overlooked as snack options.

- Hard Boiled Eggs
- Turkey slices (cold cuts)
- Popcorn with no butter. Can add seasoning such as parmesan cheese.
- Cottage Cheese (great in small glass jars)
- Cheese Slices

SMOOTHIES

Smoothies are a great option for people who are trying to gain weight/ muscle. Smoothies should not replace meals. You will want to have a smoothie along with a meal or as a snack.

BLUEBERRY AND RASPBERRY

Ingredients (1 serving = 2 cups)

- ½ cup Frozen Blueberries
- ½ cup Frozen Raspberries (can substitute any other frozen berry that you want)
- 1 cup Milk
- ¼ cup Vanilla Greek Yogurt
- 2 teaspoons Honey

Instructions

- In a blender, combine the blueberries, raspberries, Greek yogurt, milk and honey.
- Blend for a couple of minutes until a good consistency is reached.

Approximate Macronutrient Breakdown (1 serving)

Calories 265   Protein 15 g   Fat 5 g   Carbohydrates 41 g

BLUEBERRY AND SPINACH

Ingredients (1 serving = 2 cups)

- 2 cups of Frozen Blueberries
- ¼ cup fresh Spinach (rinsed well)
- ¼ cup Vanilla Greek yogurt
- 1 cup Milk
- 2 teaspoons of either Honey or Maple Syrup

Instructions

- In a blender, combine the blueberries, spinach, Greek yogurt and milk.
- Blend for a couple of minutes until a good consistency is reached.

Approximate Macronutrient Breakdown (1 serving)

Calories 300   Protein 16 g   Fat 5 g   Carbohydrates 50 g

BANANA AND PEANUT BUTTER

With this smoothie, if you are trying to mindful of your calories and carbohydrate intake or are trying to lose weight, then you can cut the recipe in half.

Ingredients (1 serving = 2 cups)

- 1 Banana
- 2 tablespoons of Peanut Butter (can substitute almond butter)
- 1 cup of Milk
- 1 teaspoon of Vanilla Extract
- 2 ice cubes
- 1 teaspoon of ground Flax

Instructions

- In a blender, combine the banana, ice cubes, peanut butter, milk, vanilla extract, and flax.
- Blend for a couple of minutes until a good consistency is reached.

Approximate Macronutrient Breakdown (1 serving)

Calories 480   Protein 23 g   Fat 22 g   Carbohydrates 52 g

BANANA AND CHERRY

Ingredients *(1 serving = 2 cups)*

- ½ Banana
- 1 cup Frozen Cherries
- ½ cup Milk
- 1/3 cup of Vanilla Greek Yogurt

Instructions

- In a blender, combine the banana, frozen cherries, milk and yogurt together.
- Blend for a couple of minutes until a good consistency is reached.

Approximate Macronutrient Breakdown (1 serving)

Calories 216   Protein 10 g   Fat 3 g   Carbohydrates 40 g

TROPICAL FRUIT

You can buy a frozen fruit pack, containing pineapple, passion fruit, and dragon fruit.

Ingredients (1 serving = 2 cups)

- 1 cup Frozen Fruit (pineapple, dragon fruit, and passion fruit)
- 1 ¼ cup Milk
- 1/3 cup Greek Vanilla Yogurt
- 1 - 2 tablespoons Honey (optional)

Instructions

- In a blender, combine the frozen fruit, milk, yogurt, and honey together.
- Blend for a couple of minutes until a good consistency is reached.

Approximate Macronutrient Breakdown (1 serving)

Calories 349   Protein 21 g   Fat 6 g   Carbohydrates 48 g

Printed in the United States
By Bookmasters